T0381374

Business, Angels, and the Natural Law of Justice

by

ABID SHAKIR

To order additional copies of this book, contact:
Xlibris
844-714-8691
www.Xlibris.com
Orders@Xlibris.com

ISBN: Softcover   978-1-4535-4674-1
        EBook   978-1-6698-1687-4

Print information available on the last page

Rev. date: 03/17/2022

ABOUT MYSELF

As a teenager, I always wanted to own my on business, but had no idea as to how to get started.

After finishing high school in 1966 I worked as a merchant seaman for two and a half years. In 1969 I was drafted into the United States Army, where I served two years; one year was spent in Vietnam as a Infantry Soldier. After serving in the military, I got a job driving tractor trailer trucks long distances. During that time, I had a continuing desire to own my own business. I thought I needed a large amount of money to get started; but realized later that was not the case.

One day while stopped at a red light, I saw a young brother crossing the street in front of me. He was very well groomed wearing a suit and bow tie. In one hand he carried newspapers, and in the other hand he held a hand carry display board with earrings for sale. I sat and watched as he approached customers in a very professional manner. The light changed, I had to move on.

About two months later while on the way to my grandmother's house just before turning into the driveway, I saw a young brother walking up the street in my direction, wearing a long white meat-butcher's coat, white shirt and bow tie, carrying boxes of frozen fish. He walked onto my grandmother's .driveway ahead of me. I got out of my car, walked slow, and followed him into the house. I quietly stood back and watched as he very professionally sold her fish. As they talked, I realized that my grandmother was a regular customer I also realized that I didn't need a lot of money to get started in business.

With creative thinking and a little money you can get started in business. When the brother finished making his sale he turned to me and invited me to come to the Muslim's temple. Before I could accept, my grandmother accepted for me. I could see it in her eyes that she wanted me to be just like this brother, because while in the army I picked up bad habits, and she was disappointed in me. I accepted his offer for the next Sunday. Sunday came, and I was ready. Brother Michael was on time. As I approached and entered the temple it was like entering a brand new world. I immediately realized I was among brave, confident brothers, that believed in do for self. It felt and sounded good, but the best was yet to come.

It was late 1975 when I began listening to the voice of Imam Warith Deen Mohammed. At that time, his name was Minister Wallace D. Mohammed. His teachings and concepts were like nothing I had heard before. He taught on the importance of prayer, the importance of root knowledge, the importance of balance and the importance of moral consciousness in business. He also taught on free thinking, spiritual vision, and much, much, more. I felt good and at peace.

I began selling Mohammed Speaks newspaper daily.

Out of that experience, I learned the art of salesmanship. I began selling eight track tapes, ladies hand bags, and jeans during the day, and kept my night job driving trucks. It was hard because I only slept a few hours between jobs.

As I drove the truck at night, I was able to listen and think on the teachings of Imam Mohammed. His teachings gave me a brand new prospective on religion, business, and life in general. I later was able to acquire a small piece of commercial property, but was not able to get a commercial loan. After ten years, my wife and I were able to payoff the property and build a small motel, that is doing very well.

PRAISE BE TO ALMIGHTY
ALLAH
(THE CREATOR)
FOR THE LEADERSHIP OF
IMAM
WARITH DEEN
MOHAMMED

Shakir Economy Motel

TABLE OF CONTENTS

About the Author...3

INTRODUCTION 8

BUSINESS..9

Keys of Development..10

ANGELS 12

THE NATURAL LAWS 14

Natural Law of Justice 15

Justice in Creation..15

Photographs and news clips 19

MY STORY 37

SUMMARY 40

INTRODUCTION

This Publication will convey the importance of business to individual and community well being. It will also explain how natural forces (angels) play such a crucial and supporting role in our world, and explain how natural laws govern and support human existence. In this attempt, I will use my own experiences in business and in life in general to explain and demonstrate the importance of business for personal and community development; and explain why I believe prayer, planning, patience and perseverance aid in this quest.

BUSINESS

The occupation of work or trade in which a person is engaged in commercial, industrial or professional dealings; the buying and selling of goods and services.

Business is a key motivating force for community progress and .growth: it reaches everyone in some form.

The motivation for trade and profit has stimulated minds and given birth to entrepreneurs for thousands of years. During those years, business at time had been misunderstood to be sinful. Honest and honorable trade for profit is not a sin.

It is reported that Allah's messenger, the Prophet Muhammad, (peace and blessing of Allah be upon him) as saying "the truthful and the trusty merchant is associated with the Prophet, the upright, and martyrs". So therefore, business is good as long as it is practiced in a honorable manner.

To be blessed with the aspiration for beginning a new business is good, but there can be problems associated with beginning a business. One problem some people run into when starting a business is expecting everything to be easy, and expecting to make a lot of money right away. Often, a new business will start slow, and will test your worthiness for the fruit you are asking it to produce. You may not realize it, but a slow start in business can be beneficial. A slow start in business forces you to thoroughly learn the business, and causes you to participate in a natural growth process. This growth process sometimes tests your patience and your desire to succeed. It may also develop your ability to respond to unseen and adverse situations. This development is very important to the business person, because as your business grow, you must grow in order to maintain your business.

This world has been designed by the creator to test us. There will always be unexpected problems and adverse situations that can interrupt your plans. Those problems act as a weeder to weed out the unable. In most cases the able will become stronger, more responsible and better equipped to handle the next hurdle of adversity.

Statistics shows that more than half of new businesses fail during the first five years of operation. New business people often under estimate the work and dedication that a new business requires. Sometimes, a business can be like a new born baby that needs a lot of care and attention for years before it is able to stand alone and move on it's own. The same principle applies, no matter how large or small the business maybe. The business person in charge should have a clear understanding and a clear concept of what he or she is trying to accomplish. A clear concept eliminates unnecessary and costly movement, and keeps all your efforts flowing in the right direction, which can be very helpful during the beginning stages. I personally have found that it is best to have backup support; another job or a existing business. This relieves some of the pressure, and allows you to get through those beginning and trying months.

IMPORTANT KEYS TOWARD RESPONSIBLE DEVELOPMENT

Prayer

Planning

Patience

Perseverance

These keys can be instrumental in developing <u>mature</u> and <u>responsible reasoning</u>.

You must pray. You have to realize that nothing happens except by the will of the Creator. Prayer is very necessary. We should also know and understand that our world has been created on a very sophisticated plan. In order for us to survive and be successful, we must plan. Business in most cases are born out of and revolve around creative planning. Creative planning in business can not be taken lightly or emphasized enough. We must also learn to be patient because successful planning in business often takes time to develop. During these stages of development we are often tested with adversity. Adversity tests your ability to persevere and stay focused on your goals. We have to realize that in business, you go through a natural growth process. When we look at the natural ·world, we see growth and development. This is the example that we, as human beings, should pattern ourselves after. We should not expect everything to be quick, easy, and just like we want it. That's just not the way of the world, so we have to accept that and learn the importance of perseverance. Persevering broadens vision and gives strength.

Patience and perseverance is important when dealing in business. Often, a business person will get frustrated because things don't appear to move fast enough. We fail to see the whole picture. True success is not just the accumulation of money, equally important is community development as well as the experience that is gained during an honorable struggle for material wealth. Often, if you come into money too quick and easy it can work against you, and can defeat a more important inner development. We can also learn a lot by observing and understanding our natural surrounding. One observation can be the natural patterns of our world. Natural patterns in nature are often reflected in human society. Patterns that offer instructive signs. When we look at the pattern of our world we see rotation and evolution. The world rotates around the sun giving us night and day, winter and summer. There is a great lesson to be learned in this. Our creator rotates the natural world and the lives of the human being. He rotates the struggles and the ease in order to test us. We also see in the natural world, growth and development in stages. When the business person sees these examples, it should strengthen his ability to persevere and endure hard times. He should say to himself; yes it maybe rough in my life now, but I understand the justice in creation, so I will patiently persevere because I know spring is coming.

But don't miss understand me; perseverance doesn't mean just sitting in one place, waiting on something to happen. Perseverance means to continue to struggle and work toward your goals. Allah (the creator) says "man will have nothing except that which he earn". Almighty Allah says in the Wholly Quran, *"to* whom much is given much is required". We as humans sometimes make the mistake take of expecting much and giving little. What we need to understand is that the criteria is set in JUSTICE and will not change, and that progress often rides on sacrifice. So realizing in the world you have to earn your way, you are not held back by <u>wishful thinking</u>. You know that in order to be successful in business as well as life in general you must be willing to work hard and make sacrifices. You must trust your own creative mind and initiative, and not be afraid of making mistakes. You should see your mistakes as a step forward and a part of your learning process. You should know and understand the importance of initiative, because the lack of initiative is one element that stops the progress of many, many people. The fear of failing and a distrust in there own creative thinking, could hinder there start in business. You should pray, plan, be patient, learn to persevere, in order to be successful. These elements are the WOMB OF SUCCESS, and never give up on the baby - SUCCESS. Though it may be a learning process, you keep trying because most often it's just the matter of prayer, planning, patience, perseverance and time.

Almighty Allah has created man to be the most powerful creature in the universe, with the ability to reason, to respond, and adjust to unexpected situations in everyday life as well as business. You must be able to respond with a creative and active mind. And know that you have been blessed with these tools to solve problems. So don't be afraid to trust and use them.

ANGELS

Forces in the natural world used by our creator to carry out his will.

In the wholly Quran almighty Allah speaks on the many different roles of his Angles, one very important role is that of Gabriel. He is the Angle assigned by Allah to bring revelation to the hearts and minds of his prophets. Another is Michael, the Angle assigned to bring inspiration to man kind. Almighty Allah also talks about the Angles Harut and Marut. They are the Angles used to test human intent. They are Angles of trial. There are times when the Angles are mentioned in the Wholly Quran by the thousands. And how our creator uses them to carry out his will. So when thinking on the Angles and their function in creation, we must first dismiss that elementary idea we were taught in elementary Sunday School. To start we must go back to a time before our creation. A time when our Creator first told the Angels he was about to create man as the ruler in creation. And they all submitted but <u>one</u>. We must expand our minds and try to grasp a fraction of the majesty of our Creator. And the function of his Angels. But there is a tendency in man to see the creation of the Angels as being above his. And even the Angels in the beginning had doubt about the creation of man; but All mighty Allah cleared up that misunderstanding by calling Adam forward. Allah said to him, "Adam tell them their names." (Explain to them their nature). When Adam told them their names, they all bowed down but <u>one</u>.

Man must remember and understand that he was favored by Allah above the rest of creation. Man was given a special gift; Almighty Allah gave man something of his own spirit, a gift that was not given to any other part of creation including Angels. Man was blessed with compassion, with the ability to reason, and with free will.

Angels come in many forms; the form of enlightenment, inspiration, sound, gravity, sight, and sometimes in the form of men and woman performing deeds of good in <u>very key</u> situations. The person being used as an angel may not realize that they are being used at that moment in the capacity of a angel. Angels come in many forms; rain, heat, drought, disease, etc... These angels have been created and commanded by the Creator to serve his will in creation. They can work against you or for you depending on your heart and intentions.

Man with all his freedom are still subject to natural law. Man often makes the mistake of thinking he can do wrong and get away with it. He fails to realize that there are natural laws in creation that will not allow it. Laws that are inforced by the angels. He fails to realize that creation is one and the dictions coming from his own heart and action, have the power to summon an angel. These angels may come in many forms, hard times, good times, disease, rain, wind, heat, drought, etc.... They may serve or work against you, depending on your own intention and action, but just because the angel may seem unfavorable at times doesn't always mean that they are working against you. Some times, hardship serves you. It grows and develops qualities that otherwise may never be developed. Often, if a person or people are faced with hardship it makes them stronger. We must respect and understand the natural laws that governs creation. Laws that are enforced by the Angels. Laws that leads to prosperity or failure, depending on actions and intentions. Angels must not be over looked because they do exist, and they do play a very important role in our lives, and assist in our success or failure. We have to REMEMBER that there was <u>one</u> among the Angels that was not an Angel. <u>One</u> that did not submit. <u>One</u> that was created in <u>dry logic</u> and did not realize his inability to reason and make decisions without the attribute of compassion. <u>One</u> that was haughty, arrogant and dared to question Allah's decision to make man the crown of creation. And when he could not get his way; asked the creator for respite (time) and vowed to lay in the path of man, to trip him up to approach him from all sides, to make wrong seems right and right seems wrong. His name is Satan (Eblis). Remember him because he never forget you.

THE

NATURAL LAW

OF

JUSTICE

Laws set in place by our creator to protect and govern.

Natural Law of Justice

To start, we need to understand that creation is based on and governed by many laws. One being the law of retribution. This law is one of the most important laws governing human intent and action. The law of retribution is a law firmly rooted in justice. A law that say's you get back what you give out. A law that is relevant in every aspect of human deeds and endeavors; but at the same time, is a law that is most often over looked because most of the time it's not respected or considered in our decision making with the urgency and the importance that it deserves. But, if we realize how precise and relevant this law is to human deeds, we would check every word parting our lips, and every intent governing our actions, because every word could be a word against your own self. And every intent behind the action could be a bridge or a pitfall against your self. The law of retribution is a law that should be respected and considered at all times in our decision making.

In the Wholly Quran all mighty Allah says that he has created this creation in just ends. There are natural laws of truth, justice, (reality) that we must respect and can not escape. We have to realize that millions of people have lived, and died by these laws for thousands of years and they won't be altered to suit our individual desires. We must learn to live by and respect these laws of justice and balance in order to realize true success. Whoever ignores the natural laws of justice working in creation may be subject to encounter hard times and not realize why. When an individual or government ignores the natural laws of justice when dealing with others, whether it be government, one on one, or what ever, they maybe subject to suffer. There are governors in this world that think they can ignore and mistreat the small man and still strive and be successful. They fail to realize that's not natural. They fail to understand that our whole creation was born out of and based on justice and balance.

 How can a man mistreat and hurt his own feet and still expect to have good mobility and balance?

 Almighty Allah has created this creation in just ends. There is a natural law of justice rooted into the foundation of the realities that governs the creation. There is no such thing as work without pay; good deeds without rewards. It may not come as we expect it sometimes but for every ounce of work or good deed done, it's registered in your own being to develop and expand your human makeup. That same bit of knowledge one day, may open the door for you to make millions. We must realize that the strength of the human being lies in his or her good human qualities, because our material achievements must first start with the vision and concepts from within. When we start doing things that are wrong and immoral we are undermining ourselves, so we must try to understand the laws that govern us and our world in order to realize greater success.

16

There are people in this world that will have you to believe <u>superstition</u>, <u>gambling</u> and <u>spooky</u> thinking leads to success; and will invite you to confuse spooky thinking with religion (that is wrong). I am told that there are some that are able to mystify the mind with things and action that seems impossible. But I am telling you, the road to success for humanity is to Allah and everyday responsibility. I don't care if someone has the power to levitate ten thousand bodies or is able to talk to the dead ten thousand times a day, none of these kinds of things aid or support human progress and development as trust in Allah, belief in his angels, respect for his laws, and the ability to deal with everyday responsibility. When those ten thousand bodies stop levitating they are going to need food to survive. Food from a farmer, someone that understands the value of responsibility; someone that understands the importance of cultivating the earth; some one that understands the law of reality; the law that says in order to survive and be successful in this world you must respect the laws that govern it. Laws that rewards responsible behavior. Laws that are as profound and PRESENT as the blood that saturates and influence our bodily function. Laws that form our minds with concepts of balance and justice through the order of our world. An order that suggests balance through organization; an order that demands planning, patience, and perseverance; an order that has it roots in the natural law of justice.

PATIENTS AND PERSEVERANCE

Wholly Quran Surah II Ayat 153, 155, 156, and 157

153.   O ye who believe! Seek help
         With patient Perseverance
         And Prayer: for Allah is with those
         Who patiently persevere.

155.   Be sure we shall test you
         With something of fear
         And hunger, some loss
         In goods or lives or the fruits
         (Of your toil), but give
         Glad tidings to those
         Who patiently persevere -

156.   Who say, when afflicted
         With calamity: "To Allah
         We belong, and to Him
         Is our return" –

157.   They are those on whom (Descend) blessings from their Lord, And Mercy, And
         They are the ones That receive guidance.

Peace and Success.

Wholly Quran Surah II Ayat 3,4, and 5.

To those who fear Allah:
who believe in the unseen,
are steadfast in prayer
and spend out of what
we have provided for them
and who believe in the
revelation
sent to thee
and sent before thy time
and (in there hearts)
have the assurance of
the hereafter.
They are on (true guidance)
from their lord. And it is
these who will prosper.

Vietnam 1969 -101st Air Born Div.

Alpha Co. 1st Platoon-1st Squad

VIETNAM was a very hard experience. To go from drinking water from clean sanitary glasses, sleeping in a warm comfortable bed, and all the other benefits taken for granted in America; to drinking water from the ground, picking leaches from your body, being wet for days during monsoon season, was an experience hard to explain. The mental pressure was even harder. The thought of not returning home was always in my subconscience if not conscience mind. Loosing a friend to a sniper bullet moments after a long conversation about going home, made me wonder if I would be next. Vietnam taught me the true meaning of fighting to survive.

A cool drink of water.

Former North Vietnamese Soldier.

Abid and Madiene Shakir

Jacksonville Masjid

When I became a Muslim under the leadership of Imam Warith Deen Mohammed, it was the most fulfilling time of my life. I was introduced to a completely different way of thinking. The Imam teachings on family, business, religion, history, and our purpose in the world, was like nothing I had heard before. It was like drinking water for the first time. I could sit for hours during the forth Sunday broadcast, without tiring. His teaching created a thurst for understanding. I know this experience altered my life for the best.

Shakir Family

Jacksonville Masjid 1982

Shakir Enterprises

The beginning days of
Shakir Enterprises was a
learning experience. One
lesson I learned, was the
importance of a good display
for retail sales.

Shakir Enterprises

Jacksonville Journal January 1985

CRAIG TRUMBO/staff

Abid Shakir displays some of his wares at the rented tent that houses half of his Shakir Enterprises at Moncrief Road and Edgewood Avenue.

Street peddler is finding business fine under tents

Eight years ago, Abid Shakir turned to Jacksonville's streets to drum up a little extra cash.

Today, he has a thriving business aptly named Shakir Enterprises.

Shakir Enterprises specializes in jeans for men and women, but also offers shirts, women's handbags and book bags. Jewelry, caps and jackets are added, depending on the season.

"It's more convenient and cheaper to display goods on the street, and I found out that people will stop and buy when they can walk by or ride by and see the items," said Shakir, who owns the business with his wife, Madiene.

For the past six months, Shakir has done most of his business under a rented 20-by-40-foot green and white tent at Moncrief Road and Edgewood Avenue.

But he still operates from his old site on Golfair Boulevard near Norwood Avenue, in an area once used as a parking lot for a department store that went out of business.

Shakir said when he started using tents, he would put them up and take them down every night at both sites. But he has made them permanent now and his profit has tripled, he said.

The tents give people the idea

Bettye Sessions

Northside

that the business is going to be around, he said.

"Another thing that helped business was when I started using professionally painted signs to advertise my sales prices," Shakir said.

He tries to stay open from 9:30 a.m. to 7:30 p.m. six days a week and has hired three part-time employees to help. Shakir and his wife work with them in the evenings and on Saturdays.

The Shakirs have other, full-time jobs. Shakir, 36, is a truck driver for American Bakeries. His wife is a paste-up artist for the Florida Publishing Co. They have an 11 year old son, Muhammads.

Shakir started his sidewalk business by selling eight-track tapes. When the tapes became difficult to get, he began peddling handbags

downtown by Hemming Park.

He said he stopped selling downtown because the police kept telling him he could not block the sidewalks and the passageways in the park.

"I made a wooden rack for the handbags and put it on top of my old Nova Chevrolet. I added jeans and kept them in the trunk of my car and started selling at the back entrance to Gateway Shopping Center," Shakir said.

"Then I got a good deal on a Kary-Dodge van in Ocala. I bought the van, brought it back to Jacksonville, added four more racks and moved to the lot on Golfair Boulevard," he said.

In the spring of 1983, Shakir bought a trailer, added five more racks and began selling at the Moncrief-Edgewood corner.

Shakir said Islamic teachings on patience and perseverance have kept him going, he said.

Mrs. Shakir said her husband began talking about starting his own business when they were dating.

"It has been a struggle, but he is a very determined person. His ultimate goal is to be his own boss," she said.

Call Bettye Sessions at 765-9736 to contribute Northside community news items.

Shakir Economy Motel 1987

I begin thinking of owning a motel during my senior year in high school, eleven years later the dream of owning a motel started to take shape. In 1977 I purchased a commercial lot at a good price; but because I had no prior experience in the hospitality industry, and a lack of collateral, I was unable to acquire a loan for the construction of the motel. After years of trying to get financing with no success, I decided to start the construction of the motel even if it took laying one block at a time. I located a general contractor that was willing to work with me. I paid the contractor a fee to draw the blueprint and to pull the building permit. I then carried the plans to a building supply company where I met with a sales person. The sales person and I were able to go over the plans and figure out the materials needed for the construction; this did not include the masonry materials. The supply company allowed me to start a lay-away of sort; I made payments on the materials for about 3 months. I then carried the blueprints to a masonry supply manufacture. Again I met with a salesperson to try to make an arrangement similar to the arrangement made with the building supply company. I was surprise when the manufacture offered me 30 day net on all masonry building supplies. That was a huge accomplishment when you consider 70% of the construction was masonry.

When the supply companies begin to deliver the building materials, I realized that this was no small project, and I needed a good PLAN to keep the project from becoming too big for me. My Jean business was doing well. I decided the best way to handle the project was to put up a security fence around the construction site and be PATIENT. I contacted sub contractors and explained my financial situation; we came up with a plan to pay on the building materials every other week, and to pay for labor every other week, this plan worked well. The construction took about 3 years to complete. Shakir Economy Motel opened for business in September 1987.

Shakir Economy Motel

The original <u>planning</u> for the first the phase of Shakir Economy Motel
included preparation for construction of the second phase.

CONSTRUCTION of Shakir Economy Motel was a challenging experience; a shortage of capital caused construction to take longer than it should have. The first phase of the motel took three years to complete. Construction of the second phase also lasted for three years; mainly because of the shortage of capital and rigged building codes of the state of Florida. The construction crew consisted of me and three other men. We performed a lot of manual labor that should have been done by crane, such as; lifting 80 trusses up two floors and placing beams with a scaffold and hand pulley. Working in those types of conditions was frustrating at times.

One day while working, a white pigeon flew into our work space as if he were trained to be around us. He showed no fear. The pigeon stayed about seven days before flying away. I said to my wife the pigeon may be a good sign of things to come. We did get better results with our building inspections and the final inspection went better that we expected. Maybe the pigeon was a good sign.

Three years of overcoming different problems and situations that I encountered during the construction, help me to better understand the value of PERSEVERANCE.

MY STORY

Beginning at the age of thirteen, I started working as a stock boy at the neighborhood grocery store. There I learned the art of work. I learned no matter how insignificant a job may seem all work takes a certain amount of strategy. Before the job at the grocery store, the only work experience I had was selling peaches door-to-door during the summer for a fruit peddler that came to our neighborhood to hire the neighborhood boys to sell his fruit. At the end of each work day the one who sold the most fruit received a cash bonus. Being the best sales boy was as important to me as the cash bonus; during that time I begin to realize my competitive spirit. The job at the grocery store paid very little, but considering the work experience and the lessons I learned about responsibilities at the age of thirteen the pay wasn't so bad. During that time I also realized I liked to dress. I wanted the nice clothes that I saw the older boys wearing. It wasn't long before my friends began to comment on my style of dressing. I didn't realize that I was dressing well enough to be notice. My grandmother was very supportive of me, encouraging me to stay on the job when I started complaining about the difficulties at work; she made sure that my converse tennis shoes were cleaned (snow white) every morning for school. My shirts were so welled laundered that everyone thought I was having my shirts professionally done. My grandmother meant a lot to me and I did not want to disappoint her in anyway.

Being employed at an early age gave me more freedom to come and go with less restriction. I liked going to the movies with my friends. With this new freedom I started hanging out on the street corners with my friends when I wasn't working. Hanging out on the street corner allowed me to meet new friends. One day while hanging out, a new friend mention a job that he was thinking about quieting, the job was downtown at a popular steak house restaurant. I asked him to let me have the job at the steak house as a dish washer he replied that he would speak to the owner. I got the job. The work was very challenging because the restaurant had very good business and I was the only dish washer. The work hours added to the difficulties, I started work after school and I left work at 12 midnight; and up for school the next morning at 6:00 a.m. My father was a taxicab driver at night, so transportation to or from work was never a problem.

I lived with my aunt and grandmother. My aunt was an elementary school teacher, my grandmother was retired, and they allowed me to spend my money as I pleased. I spent most of my salary on school clothes. I love my aunt and grandmother very much but my mother was my heart. She, my father, brother and three sisters lived on the other side of town. They seemed to be having it hard when I visited them and often times I would leave feeling very sad. Sometimes I found myself PRAYING that the creator would help me to help them. I learned the value of prayer at an early age because my aunt was very religious. She would have prayer meetings two or three times a week in our home, she also led a Gospel singing group; in that environment prayer was familiar to me.

I worked at the restaurant for about two years. One day during my senior year I was in the school library and over heard the librarian speaking to someone about a job at a nursing home for the elderly. After she finished speaking with the person I asked her how much the job pays. The pay was more than what I was making at the restaurant, so I asked her to help me get the job and she replied ok. I applied for and got the job. The work hours were the same as the work hours at the steak house restaurant. The job at the nursing home was a very sobering experience; I got alone with the patients and co-workers very well, but what I didn't realized when I begin working there was how familiar I would become with death. Sometime I would become attached to some of the patients and not long after they would pass. One night while working alone one of the men patient call me to his bed side and quietly asked me to take his life, I just walked away, I never forgot the expression on his face. He was very unhappy about his condition.

When I finished high school I started working part time at the Jacksonville Shipyard. A friend told me about a ship that was being built at that yard and how many jobs would be available when the ship was completed. He also told me how to get in touch with the ship clerk and apply for a job as a seaman after the completion of the ship. The construction of the ship would last for 6 more months. I was very persistent during those 6 months to be hired; one day the ship clerk told me that when the construction of the ship is complete I would be the first one that he hires. He kept his word.

When I begin working as a seaman for the United Stated Coast and Geodetic Survey, I did not realize how special the ship the Discoverer was or how special her role was. The ship Discoverer and her sister ship the Oceanographer was vessels used by V.I.P. scientist in the Atlantic and Pacific Ocean in the study of Oceanography. I was hired to work in the galley. The pay was good; the chief steward seemed to like my work. The only travel experience I had at that point was to Georgia with my uncle. When the Discoverer started on her maiden voyage I was very excited because my dream of being a seaman was coming true. But what I did not realize was how rough sea sickness could be. When the ship started up the St. Johns River and entered the break waters of the Atlantic Ocean, my excitement started to fade and the misery of sea sickness started to take hold. The maiden voyage was to Baltimore Maryland two days away. The Discoverer was new and not yet balanced properly, and neither was I. The two days to Maryland was two of the most miserable days of my life to that point. When the Discoverer docked in Maryland the excitement of being a seaman returned. During the ship stay, there were long lines of people almost every day touring the ship. The Discoverer was state of the art for its time. After about 3 weeks the ship returned to Jacksonville and the next voyage was to Montreal Canada, were the ship was to be on exhibition for seven days at the world fair expo 67. All of this was very exciting to me; I was able to save most of the money I made. When I returned home I was able to make a down payment on a new home for my parents, but in order for me to get the financing, my name had to be on the deeds because approval of the loan was based on my job. The builder informed me and my parents that I had to have my disabilities removed in order for my name to be included on the deeds. To have my disabilities removed we had to go before a judge; the order read "Oscar Powell Jr. is now hereby able to sue or be sued, contract or be contracted with as if he was 21 years of age." And in a matter of 10 minutes I went from a 19 year old boy to a 21 year old man; and I started to wonder was this a good thing or not.

After one year of work on the U.S. Discoverer I had enough sea time to apply at the U.S. Coast Guard for a merchant seaman document. Approval for the application took about 30 days. I began working on merchant ships out of the Jacksonville, Florida port. Shipping out of the port of Jacksonville was good, but the New Orleans port was better because work was more plentiful, so I started commuting from Jacksonville to New Orleans for work. In the 1960's most young men were concern about the war in Vietnam and I was no different. The Jacksonville draft board tried to contact me to take a physical exam on two earlier dates but each time I was out of the country working as a seaman. The draft board began sending threaten letters to my home. My mother and grandmother urged me to return home to take the physical exam to determine my draft status. I passed the exam and soon after I was drafted into the U.S. Army. I was sent to Fort Benny Georgia for basic training. After eight weeks of basic training I had to report to Fort Polk in Louisiana (Tiger Land), where I receive infantry training; Tiger Land was very rough but that was nothing compared to what was coming next. After graduation from Fort Polk, (I graduated in the top 3 in my company, and was classified as an expert shooter.) our company captain informed us that the entire company was going to Vietnam after one month furlough. The month home with my family before being deployed to Vietnam was very hard. There was a silent fear within the family. We all tried to be optimistic about my deployment, but being optimistic was almost impossible, because there were so much sad news in the country about Vietnam. The thirty days quickly passed and it was time for me to get started on my long journey to Vietnam. I said good bye to my family, my brother drove me to the air port; I boarded a plane to Oakland California to be process for Nam. During the processing time which took 3 days I felt alone and fearful of what was to come.

The flight over the Pacific Ocean to Vietnam took about 18 hours; 18 hours never pass so fast. The commercial plane that carried us to Vietnam was the last feeling of safety for the next 12 months. After the arrival to Vietnam, it took one week to process in. After receiving our individual orders we started to our destinations. None of my friends were going my way. My destination was L, Z, Sally, 101st Airborne Division where the adversary was not the Vietcong but the North Vietnamese Army; not Charlie but Mr. Charles. It was 1969 and Vietnam was a hot bed. Charles was small in stature and was not to be taken lightly. It was the beginning of the hardness year of my life, danger was all around. One of the keys of survival was to be very alert at all times. Living conditions in the jungle of Vietnam was very hard to bear especially during monsoon season were it rains continuously. Proper care of your feet was a job because trench feet and leaches were a common problem. After 8 months of hell, it was my turn to go on R&R (rest and recuperation). I chose to go to Bangkok Thailand for a week. That one week was a big relief. That week passed too fast and it was time to go back to the bush of Vietnam. I had four more months to try to stay alive. When I made it back to the bush all hell broke loose; we were in fights almost every day. Those last four months were nerve racking; the closer one came to going home, It was common to become jumpy because the thought in the back of your mind was, I've came this far and I don't want to make a mistake now. The day finally came for me to leave the bush. The terrain we were in at the time was too rough for the chopper that was transporting me out to land. The chopper hovered about 7 feet up; I had to jump to grab a ski on the chopper to pull myself into the chopper. I was finally headed home with only a piece of shrapnel from a grenade lodged in my stomach from a fire fight 6 months earlier.

Processing out of Vietnam took about one week; the day came for me to board the commercial air line to start home. When I boarded the plane I realized that I knew almost everyone on the plane. I didn't know that you leave Nam with the same soldiers that you entered with; it was like a reunion of old friends. We served in different parts of the country and we are going home together. When the plane lifted we all were very happy, but soon after we realized that there were a lot of soldiers missing, they had gone on earlier one way or the other. Some of us knew what happened to the different ones that were missing. Our conversation the rest of the way home was both happy and sad. The plane landed in California I was home at last.

SUMMARY

This publication attempted to convey the importance of a wholesome respect for our creator, his angles, and the natural laws that governs our world and the importance of business to community and personal development.

Most of the times when we are thinking of money and success we never consider the natural laws, we never consider the natural forces (angles), we often overlook the importance of PRAYER, PATIENTS and PERSEVERANCE and how these disciplines support and assist our development.

Printed in the United States
by Baker & Taylor Publisher Services